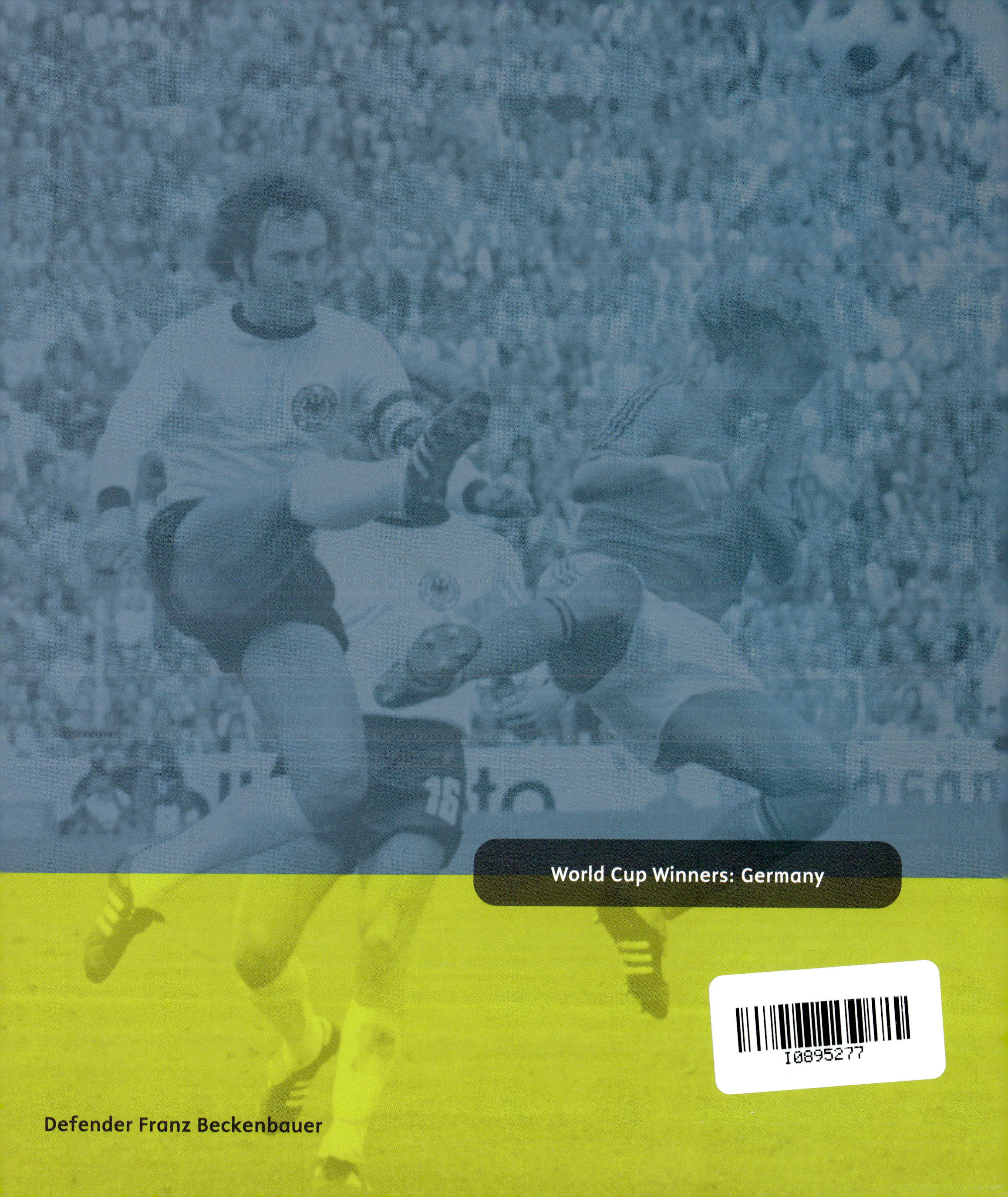

World Cup Winners: Germany

Defender Franz Beckenbauer

Striker Jürgen Klinsmann

WORLD CUP WINNERS

GERMANY

JASON OLSON

CREATIVE SPORTS

CREATIVE EDUCATION / CREATIVE PAPERBACKS

Published by Creative Education and Creative Paperbacks
P.O. Box 227, Mankato, Minnesota 56002
Creative Education and Creative Paperbacks are imprints of
The Creative Company
www.thecreativecompany.us

Book design by Blue Design (www.bluedes.com)

Images by Getty Images/AFP, 24, Andreas Gebert/picture alliance, 6, Bettmann, 1, Duffy/Allsport/Hulton Archive, 19, George Tiedemann, 2, Horstmüller/ullstein bild, 15, Jamie McDonald, 16, Jan Pitman, 3, 10, PEDRO UGARTE, 20, Stefan Matzke - sampics, cover, 7; Unsplash/Ashley Knedler, 9; Wikimedia Commons/ETH Library, 4, Herbert Behrens / Anefo, 12, IER89 7, 5

Library of Congress Cataloging-in-Publication Data
Names: Olson, Jason, 1981– author.
Title: Germany / Jason Olson.
Description: Mankato, Minnesota : Creative Education and Creative Paperbacks, 2026. | Series: Creative sports. World Cup winners | Includes index. | Audience: Ages 7–10 | Audience: Grades 2–3 | Summary: "Germany has won four FIFA World Cups, and finished second, third, or fourth in several other World Cups. This elementary title follows "Die Mannschaft" as they kick their way into soccer history"– Provided by publisher.
Identifiers: LCCN 2024046136 (print) | LCCN 2024046137 (ebook) | ISBN 9798889896029 (library binding) | ISBN 9781682777688 (paperback) | ISBN 9798889896821 (ebook)
Subjects: LCSH: Soccer–Germany–History–Juvenile literature. | World Cup (Soccer)–History–Juvenile literature.
Classification: LCC GV944.G3 O57 2026 (print) | LCC GV944.G3 (ebook) | DDC 796.334/630943–dc23/eng/20241211
LC record available at https://lccn.loc.gov/2024046136
LC ebook record available at https://lccn.loc.gov/2024046137

Printed in India

Striker Gerd Müller

Midfielder Toni Kroos

CONTENTS

Home of the Team

Germany is a large country in western Europe. It stretches from the Alps Mountains to the Baltic Sea. The Black Forest contains the source of the Danube River. It's one of Europe's longest rivers.

Germans love soccer, and for good reason. Their national team is one of the few teams to have won the World Cup. The World Cup is a worldwide soccer tournament. Countries make teams of their best players. Every four years, they compete to become world champion.

Goalkeeper Oliver Kahn

Team Traditions

Germans call their national team "Nationalelf" ("National Eleven") or "Die Mannschaft" ("The Team"). It's known for its physical playstyle. The Netherlands and Italy are some of its **rivals**.

Fans take to the streets to cheer on the team on their way to games. Many of them wear face paint and costumes. Fans who cannot make it to the stadium may host grill parties.

Forward Helmut Rahn

Team History

From 1945 to 1990, West Germany and East Germany had their own teams. West Germany won the 1954 World Cup. Its **underdog** team beat the **favorite** Hungary 3–2. Helmut Rahn scored the winning goal in "The Miracle of Bern."

The "Game of the Century" was a wild 4–3 semifinal loss to Italy in the 1970 World Cup. Five of the seven goals came in extra time. West Germany captured the 1974 World Cup title on home soil, with a 2–1 win over the Netherlands.

At the 1990 World Cup, West Germany won its third title. It defeated Argentina 1–0. It was the German team's third straight final. Its captain Lothar Matthäus would appear in a record 150 matches, collecting 23 goals.

Midfielder Lothar Matthäus (right)

Midfielder Mario Götze (left) and forward Thomas Müller (right)

GERMANY

After 1990, Germany competed as one team. In 2014, it became the first European team to win a World Cup in the Americas. It defeated Argentina 1–0 in the final. Mario Götze scored the winner in extra time—in the 113th minute! To reach the final, Germany defeated host country Brazil 7–1. It was a huge win for Germany and a crushing loss for its rival.

Team Stars

Germany has had many stars in its history. Franz Beckenbauer (called "Der Kaiser" or "The Emperor") is the only defender to win two **Ballon d'Ors**. He is one of only three people to win the World Cup as both player and coach. Striker Gerd Müller scored 68 goals in 62 **caps**. His 14 goals in World Cup matches were a record that stood for 32 years.

Defender Franz Beckenbauer

Striker Miroslav Klose

GERMANY

Miroslav Klose is Germany's all-time leading scorer (71 goals in 137 caps). He also holds the record for most goals scored in World Cups, with 16 goals across four tournaments. Oliver Kahn is the only goalkeeper to win the **Golden Ball**. Young players hope to win another World Cup for Germany soon.

About the Germany National Team

First year: 1908

Team colors: white, black, red, gold

Home stadium: various (including Olympiastadion, Alianz Arena, and Signal Iduna Park)

WORLD CUP VICTORIES:

1954, 3–2 over Hungary

1974, 2–1 over the Netherlands

1990, 1–0 over Argentina

2014, 1–0 over Argentina

WEBSITE:

https://www.dfb.de/en/home

Glossary

Ballon d'Or—an award given every year to the world's best soccer player

cap—an official match played for a national soccer team

favorite—a team that is expected to win

Golden Ball—an award given to the best player in the World Cup

rival—a team that plays extra hard against another team

underdog—a team that is not expected to win

Striker Gerd Müller

Index